5/10

D1465857

BATTLES
THAT CHANGED THE WORLD

Epidamnus

T h r a c e

Byzantium

Macedon

Strymon R.

Amphipolis

Abdera

Hebrus R.

Thasos

Olynthus

Samothrace

Aegospotami

Hellespont

Cyzicus

Thessaly

Potidaea

Sestos

Lampsacus

Scione

Abydos

Lemnos

Troy

Sigeum

Corcyra

Magnesia

Iolcus

Pherae

Pagasae

Aegean

Lesbos

Aeolis

Ambracia

Acheron R.

Artemisium

Sea

Mytilene

Lydia

Leucas

Acarnania

Aetolia

Thermopylae

Euboea

Scyros

Cyme

Sardis

Cephallenia

Delphi

Phocis

Phocaea

Ithaca

Naupactus

Corinthian Gulf

Boeotia

Chalcis

Chios

Clazomenae

Sicyon

Thebes

Delium

Erythrae

Teos

Ionia

Zacynthos

Elis

Corinth

Athens

Samos

Ephesus

Peloponnese

Mycenae

Saronic

Attica

Ceos

Delos

Argos

Gulf

Troizen

Paros

Naxos

Miletus

Caria

Ionian

Alpheius R.

Pylos

Sparta

Siphnos

Halicarnassus

Sphacteria →

Sea

Gytheum

Melos

Cos

Cnidus

Thera

Rhodes

Cythera

Carpathus

N

0   50   100   150 miles

BATTLES
THAT CHANGED THE WORLD

MARATHON

DAVID J. CALIFF

Marion Carnegie Library
206 S. Market St
Marion, IL 62959

CHELSEA HOUSE PUBLISHERS
PHILADELPHIA

FRONTIS: This map shows the mainland of ancient Greece (left) and the western coast of Asia Minor.

CHELSEA HOUSE PUBLISHERS

EDITOR IN CHIEF Sally Cheney
DIRECTOR OF PRODUCTION Kim Shinners
CREATIVE MANAGER Takeshi Takahashi
MANUFACTURING MANAGER Diann Grasse

STAFF FOR MARATHON

EDITOR Lee Marcott
PICTURE RESEARCHER Patricia Burns
PRODUCTION ASSISTANT Jaimie Winkler
COVER AND SERIES DESIGNER Keith Trego
LAYOUT 21st Century Publishing and Communications, Inc.

©2002 by Chelsea House Publishers,
a subsidiary of Haights Cross Communications.
All rights reserved. Printed and bound in the United States of America.

http://www.chelseahouse.com

First Printing

1 3 5 7 9 8 6 4 2

Library of Congress Cataloging-in-Publication Data

Califf, David J.
    Marathon / David J. Califf.
        p. cm. — (Battles that changed the world)
Include bibliographical references and index.
Summary: Presents the story of the battle of Marathon, a landmark battle in ancient history.
    ISBN 0-7910-6679-7 (alk. paper)
    1. Marathon, Battle of, 490 B.C. —Juvenile literature. 2. Greece—Civilization—To 146 B.C.—
Juvenile literature. 3. Iran—History—To 640 A.D.—Juvenile literature. [1. Marathon,
Battle of, 490 B.C. 2. Greece—Civilization—To 146 B.C. 3. Iran—History—To 640 A.D.]
I. Title. II. Series.
DF225.4 .C35 2002
938'.03—dc21

                                                          2001047727

CONTENTS

The Greeks and the Persians

The Parthenon was built on the Acropolis above the city of Athens. This temple was constructed in the fifth century B.C.E., during a period of great prosperity in Greece.

In the year 490 B.C.E., almost two-and-a-half millennia ago, 10,000 Greek citizen-soldiers assembled on a plain near Marathon, a village about 26 miles northeast of Athens. Their objective was a simple one: to block the Persian king Darius in his first attempt to add their homeland to his ever-widening kingdom. In short, they fought to preserve their freedom and way of life.

The prospect of success must have seemed bleak, for the Greeks faced a professionally trained army at least twice as large as theirs and backed by the might of an empire so vast that its capital, Susa, was a three-month journey away. Although no Greek had ever faced a Persian on the battlefield before, the eastern army's success against other enemies was well known and must have inspired a certain measure of awe, if not outright fear.

The poet Aeschylus was among the soldiers who fought at Marathon, but even he, with all his poetic imagination, could not have envisioned at the time that the Greeks would "crush the huge and shining army" of the east. These memorable words from his prizewinning play, *The Persians*, capture something of the spirit that victory at Marathon stirred in Athens, where the battle seemed to have "changed the world" even within the lifetimes of the soldiers who fought there.

How did the Greeks come to regard the Battle of Marathon as one of the most important single events in their emerging national history? Why did they treasure it above other, more militarily significant victories? What brought them to Marathon in the first place? What difference did it make in fifth-century Athens, and why should it matter today? To answer these questions and grasp the full significance of this ancient conflict and its relevance to the modern world, it helps to know something of the historical context in which the battle was waged.

In the years leading up to Marathon, "Greece" did not yet exist as a nation—at least not in the sense we understand the term today. Rather, a series of independent city-states dotted the Greek mainland, the Peloponesus, Asia Minor, and islands throughout the Aegean. The peoples of these city-states were united by a common language (although they spoke in different dialects), a free and open trade policy, and a loosely shared cultural heritage. At one time, most of the city-states had been ruled by their leading aristocratic families, who passed control from generation to generation. Then a series of nonhereditary rulers called *tyrannoi* (which led to the word "tyrant" since most were oppressive and authoritarian) began to gain and exert power. Gradually, these tyrannoi were replaced by democratic governments, and soon the ideals of democracy and

As chief magistrate in 594 B.C.E., Solon instituted reforms to calm the turmoil and to further the ideals of democracy and freedom in Greek society.

freedom (at least for freeborn, citizen males) became part of the glue that held these otherwise independent Greek states together against the forces of empire.

For many cities, the precise path of democratic revolution is difficult to document, but for Athens a remarkably good historical record exists. In 594 B.C.E. Solon was elected *archon,* or chief magistrate. With a mandate to bring the city out of a period of political and economic turmoil, he instituted several major reforms. First, he canceled all debts and freed all citizens who had been enslaved because of debt. Second, he shifted the qualification for office from noble birth to personal wealth, and although the new requirements were not fully inclusive, they nevertheless considerably increased the pool of eligible officeholders. Third, the Assembly was expanded to include all citizens regardless of class and served as the city's primary legislative body. Finally, a second council was formed as a check on the authority of the Areopagus, a powerful governing board made up of ex-magistrates. This second council consisted of 400 citizens, 100 from each tribe, and it helped set the agenda for meetings of the Assembly and served as a "voice of the people" in election planning and other official business.

Solon's reforms marked a turning point in Athenian history, but the movement toward democracy was briefly challenged by the emergence of the tyrant Pisistratus, a relative of Solon. Pisistratus seized the Acropolis and employed mercenaries to enforce his will, but he stopped short of dismantling the democratic measures that Solon had put in place. Instead, he used bribery and strong-arm tactics to manipulate elections, control magistrates, and implement his policies while appearing to work within the existing constitutional framework. Still, several noble families were displeased with his conduct. He was forced into exile twice, and twice he was able to restore the tyranny.

Upon the death of Pisistratus, his eldest son, Hippias, took power. During Hippias's reign, which was harsher and more despotic than that of his father, the rival Alcmaeonid family was forced from Athens. They attempted to return by force, first in 512 and then again in 511 with the help of a small naval force from Sparta, another powerful city-state. When both attacks failed, the ambitious Alcmaeonids tried a different approach. The sanctuary of Apollo at Delphi had recently been burned, and the Alcmaeonids took a leading role in its reconstruction. The rebuilding of the sanctuary was accompanied by graft and corruption. The Alcmaeonids allegedly siphoned off some funds to strengthen their army, and they managed to manipulate the Delphic oracle to pressure Sparta to "free Athens first" from Pisistratid tyranny. The Spartans, for their part, were still smarting over the naval defeat of 511, and in 510 they launched a more massive attack that eventually succeeded in deposing Hippias. Because they had been instructed by the oracle to "free Athens," the Spartans could not very well maintain control of the rival city, as they might have liked, but in return for their aid, they did demand that Athens join the Spartan-led Peloponesian League. For generations to come, Sparta would remain a major force to be reckoned with.

After the tyrant had been expelled, leadership of Athens was contested between the ex-archon Cleisthenes, an Alcmaeonid, and Isagoras, supported by the family of the deposed Hippias, who was determined to regain control and who would continue irritate Athens until his death. When Isagoras was elected archon in 508, Cleisthenes had only one chance of regaining power: a direct appeal to the people. In the Assembly, he proposed and passed a series of democratic reforms and effectively limited the power of Isagoras. The Spartan king Cleomenes, a personal friend of Isagoras, agreed to send troops to expel Cleisthenes from Athens, but the Athenian people were not about to tolerate further Spartan interference. A mass uprising was able to check the attack and restore Cleisthenes to power.

These experiences revealed to Cleisthenes a weakness in the democratic system of Solon, in which powerful families still retained considerable influence. To combat this problem, Cleisthenes abolished the four old tribes, which were based on blood relation, and replaced them with ten new tribes based on geography. Solon's 400-member council was replaced by a new council of 500, to which each new tribe contributed 50 members. The council of Cleisthenes was a successful exercise in representative democracy and expanded upon the responsibilities of Solon's council. While the direct democracy of the Assembly still retained the authority to legislate, the details of proposed legislation were typically worked out by the council, whose recommendations the Assembly often followed. By 508, then, the full machinery of democracy was established in Athens, and its citizens were prepared to fight to preserve it, for each tribe also contributed foot soldiers and cavalry to a standing army.

While Athens and other Greek city-states were struggling to establish stable democratic governments, several decidedly undemocratic kingdoms were competing for supremacy in the east. By the middle of the 7th century B.C.E., the kingdom of Assyria had established itself as the leading power of the Near and Middle East. Based in Ninevah, on the banks of the Euphrates River in modern-day Iraq, the Assyrian empire stretched from Egypt through Palestine, Syria, and eastern Turkey, and extended eastward through Iraq and into western Iran. To the east of Assyria was the kingdom of Media, which reached all the way to the plain of Bactria in modern Afghanistan. To the south of Assyria and Media was the smaller kingdom of Babylonia. Throughout the late 600s, the Medes found themselves at odds with the Assyrians, and toward the end of the century they formed an alliance with the Babylonians, attacked the city of Ninevah in 612, and broke up the Assyrian empire. The southwestern region came under Babylonian control while the heart of Assyria (Iraq) and the eastern part of Asia Minor (Turkey) were controlled by Media.

Based in Sardis at the western end of Asia Minor, the kingdom of Lydia was also flourishing at this time, and it often held skirmishes with the Medes to prevent them from expanding westward. By 560 B.C.E., Lydia was controlled by Croesus, who brought the Greek states of Aeolia and Ionia on the Turkish coast under Lydian control. Croesus, however, was a lover of all things Greek, and Greek influence quickly spread throughout Lydia. The Lydians, in return, gave Greece, and by extension the modern world, one of the

Cyrus the Great of Persia overthrew the government of Croesus in
Lydia, thereby exposing Greece to hostile eastern forces.

most enduring elements of human civilization: coins.
Indeed, Croesus was a man of extraordinary wealth and
power, and he was equally generous to his friends and
savage to his enemies. It is thought that Croesus wanted to
capture the Greek mainland and that he might have
succeeded were it not for an emerging threat from the east.

Cyrus the Great, a Persian (Iranian) of the Achaemenid
family, was building a power base of his own. Having

captured the throne of Media, he went on to sack Sardis and depose Croesus in 546 B.C.E.. The life of Croesus was apparently spared, and two stories (both probably false) emerged to explain his fate. The first is found in a poem by Bacchylides, who writes that "when Zeus had fulfilled his fated destiny, and Sardis had been sacked by the Persian host, Apollo of the golden sword saved Croesus, the king of horse-taming Lydia." Croesus, not wanting to live a life of slavery at the hands of a Persian master, built a funeral pyre and planned to burn himself alive. The poet continues,

> His maiden daughters shrieked
> and cast their dear hands
>
> to their mother. Death foreseen
> is the worst slaughter of all.
>
> But when the flashing force
> of the horrible flame leapt,
>
> then Zeus sent a black-
> cloaking cloud to quench
>
> the red-orange blaze.
> Nothing is past belief
>
> when fashioned by gods' concern.
> Then Delian Apollo
>
> carried the old man
> to the land of the Hyperboreans
>
> and settled him there together
> with his delicate-ankled daughters
>
> because of his piety.

Herodotus, an ancient Greek historian, offers an equally incredible tale. In his version, it is Cyrus who condemned Croesus to the burning pyre. While the flames were rising, Croesus called out the name of Solon, the Athenian statesman who had allegedly paid a visit to Sardis

Herodotus: Father of History

Herodotus of Halicarnassus was born in 485 B.C.E., an age when "history" did not yet exist either as a genre of writing or as a systematic study of human affairs unfolding in time. Stories and legends of a distant past were commonplace, first in oral traditions and later in written forms, but little effort was made to distinguish the myths of epic, often couched in the language of poetry, from empirical fact. The rise of science and philosophy in the sixth and fifth centuries, however, helped foster an interest in current events and a desire to study the past in a more rational, objective, and systematic way. Hecataeus of Miletus was one of the first writers to study the people and regions of his own day, but his interests ultimately had more to do with geography than history.

A generation later, Herodotus combined the research program of Hecataeus (indeed, *historia* means "investigation") with the narrative writing style he had learned from Homeric epic, but he wrote in prose and without the embellishments of poetic art. He traveled extensively for 17 years, meeting people in dozens of countries, gathering stories, and taking copious notes. The idea that recent events were worthy of scientific study was relatively new, and Herodotus was one of its pioneers. His method was simple: first to research what happened during the last hundred years through written records, oral tales, and personal observation, and then to report his findings in the form of an organized, continuous story. In this sense, he was the first true historian of the Western world.

To be sure, Herodotus's *Histories* have certain faults. He sometimes made up details or creatively imagined what might have happened when he could not find the facts. In other instances, he was too quick to believe unreliable sources and included errors of fact that could have been avoided by more careful checking. Religious superstition sometimes led him to pay too much attention to prophecies, omens, and dreams. He also had a tendency to exaggerate and at times slanted his history (perhaps understandably) in favor of the Greeks. In addition, Herodotus's narrative tended to lack the kind of analysis expected from historical writing, and the analysis he included does not always seem true.

Herodotus: Father of History (cont.)

For all these shortcomings, however, Herodotus was a brilliant writer. He was a thoughtful and curious observer of human affairs who tried to understand not merely what people do but how their personalities and life experiences guide their actions. He saw the value of historical context, that is, the way events build on one another and how such things as culture, geography, politics, and religion influence those events. He was a conscientious researcher who strove to be thorough and honest. Above all, Herodotus knew a good story when he heard one, and his ability as an engaging storyteller is unmatched.

many years before. (The chronology is all but impossible since Solon's archonship had occurred 34 years before Croesus even came to power.) As the story goes, Croesus had asked Solon if, in all his travels, he ever came across "anyone who was happier than everyone else." The wealthy and powerful Croesus expected Solon to name *him* as the happiest of men, but instead Solon replied that "human life is a matter of chance" and that no man should be considered happy "until he is dead," for good fortune can quickly turn into bad. Upon hearing the story, Cyrus was so moved that he ordered the flames to be extinguished, but it was too late. The fire was out of control. As if borrowing from the account of Bacchylides, Herodotus then reports that Croesus called upon Apollo to rescue him from danger. "Suddenly the clear, calm weather was replaced by gathering clouds; a storm broke, rain lashed down, and the pyre was extinguished."

The fact that Croesus appeared so frequently in Greek art and literature only underscores the important role that his kingdom played in the development of Greece. For many years, Lydia had served as a buffer for Greece

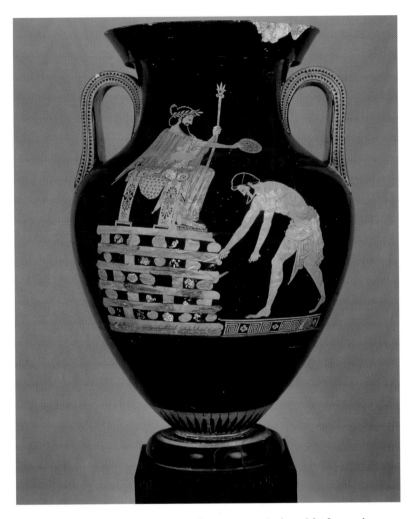

This ancient Greek vase shows Croesus seated on his funeral pyre.

against the more hostile eastern kingdoms of which they had practically no knowledge. With the rise of the Persian empire, that buffer was removed, and Greek history entered an entirely new phase: a 67-year struggle with an empire of such size and might that it dwarfed the Greek world by comparison.

Once Lydia was firmly under Persian control, Cyrus proceeded to subdue the Greek cities of Aeolia and Ionia, previously controlled by Croesus. He imposed a system of annual taxation and occasionally compelled Greek soldiers to serve in the Persian army. Although the Aeolians and Ionians had been generally, if reluctantly, compliant with Croesus's Lydia, they were more resistant to Persian rule and decided to ask Sparta to intervene on their behalf. The Spartans refused. Soon Cyrus strengthened his hold on the region with the conquest of Babylon and, after his death, his son Cambyses captured Egypt.

A rebellion at home called Cambyses back from Egypt, but he soon fell victim to a man posing as his brother, Smerdis, whom the new king had condemned to death for disloyalty. This impostor bore a striking resemblance to the real Smerdis—in fact, some modern historians believe that he was the real Smerdis—and he almost succeeded in his attempt to seize power. When Cambyses died on the way to Susa under suspicious circumstances ("by his own hand," according to one report), the legitimate heir to the Persian throne was a man named Hystaspes; however, Hystaspes lacked the will and the resources needed to challenge "Smerdis," who had successfully established a strong base of support. Unhappy with this state of affairs, Darius, the son of Hystaspes, formed an alliance with other noblemen and was soon able to take power for himself. To secure his hold on the kingdom, Darius married Atossa, the widow of Cambyses, herself a daughter of Cyrus.

Despite the emerging presence of democracies and an aversion to foreign domination, there was also some pressure in the Greek cities for détente with Persia. Three main political forces were in play: the proponents of democracy, local tyrants and other powerful families favoring home rule under their leadership, and the Persian king and his family. Often, the interests of the last two groups intersected: Tyrants sought Persian military assistance to help them maintain their own power while the Persians, through a system of political patronage, sought help from leading Greek families who had lost influence through the creation of democratic institutions. Such was the state of affairs in the region when Darius decided to mount his first great European campaign.

In 513 B.C.E. the Persian king marched his army into Thrace where he met with great success, as far as can be seen from the few historical records that survive. Part of the mission—the main part, if the fanciful account of Herodotus is to be believed—was to attack the Scythians, a people of southern Russia who had successfully waged war against Media a century before. After building a bridge over the Danube River, the Persian king left a detachment of Ionian and Aeolian Greeks to guard the bridge against the Scythians, who might try to destroy it and thereby cut off the Persians' return home. Among the Greek leaders was Miltiades, son of Cimon. When the Scythians arrived at the bridge, they proposed to the Ionians that their two peoples should join forces against the Persians and ultimately free the Greeks from Persian imperial control. Miltiades was in favor of the proposal and advocated the destruction of the bridge, but Histiaeus of Milteus was able to persuade the other Ionian commanders to remain loyal to Darius, who could guarantee them continued positions of power in return. To appease the Scythians, Histiaeus pretended to cooperate and destroyed part of the bridge, only to replace it when Darius arrived.

Whether this mission to Thrace was planned as a prelude to the invasion of mainland Greece cannot be known with certainty. It is possible that Darius only meant to secure his northern frontier. Whatever the intent, however, it is clear that his move got the attention of the Greeks.

Prelude to Marathon

The palace and audience hall of the Persian king Darius I has reliefs depicting Persian guards and a lion attacking a bull. The palace was built in 518-460 B.C.E., during the Achaemenian period.

After Darius's expedition in Thrace, there was a growing fear among the Greeks that their own freedom and security might be threatened by a Persian invasion. An equally unacceptable alternative was rule by local tyrants, many of them supported by Persia, who blocked all democratic efforts from flowering. Among these tyrants was Histiaeus of Miletus, the pro-Persian general of the Scythian campaign. Histiaeus was rewarded by the Persian king with the governorship of Myrcinus, a land rich in natural resources, notably silver and wood. Unfortunately for the tyrant, Megabazus, a Persian general, wanted control of the region—and its wealth— for himself, so he successfully persuaded Darius to summon the

Greek to the court at Susa where he might serve as a "special adviser." Aristagoras, the son of Histiaeus, was left to govern Miletus, their native town.

Meanwhile, there was a democratic revolt on the island of Naxos, which resulted in the expulsion of some of its leading aristocratic families. The exiles fled to Aristagoras for aid and were reassured that Naxos could be reclaimed with Persian support, but when a Persian commander arrogantly boasted of his plan to capture the island, the Naxians fortified their homeland and were able to withstand the attack.

Aristagoras became angry with the Persians for spoiling his designs on greater power, so he switched sides and became an advocate of democratic revolution. He gave up the tyranny of Miletus and encouraged other tyrants to do likewise. He then approached Sparta, Athens, and Eretria for assistance. The Spartans refused, but the Athenians and Eretrians agreed and joined the Ionians in an attack on Sardis, the seat of Persian power in Asia Minor. The city was leveled, but the Athenians lost a subsequent sea battle with the Persians, and as a result they withdrew from the revolt. Aristagoras was killed while fleeing to Thrace.

Back in Susa, Histiaeus managed to persuade Darius that he should be allowed to return to Ionia to help calm the uprising. When he got to Sardis, however, the father of Aristagoras was greeted by a hostile Artaphernes, *satrap* (provincial governor) of the destroyed city, so he fled to Chios and took up the cause of revolution. Indeed, Histiaeus even claimed that the revolt was his idea in the first place, a ploy to get back home. He began to spread the story that he had sent a slave from Susa to Miletus with a message urging his son to action. To avoid detection by the Persians, the incriminating message was allegedly branded into the slave's head and then concealed by the growth of hair, which could be shaved off to reveal the message upon meeting Aristagoras. Whether or not this story is true cannot be known, but it is clear that Histiaeus had lost all favor with the Persians. He was hunted down and crucified by Artaphernes, who went on to sack the city of Miletus. Soon the rebellion was crushed.

The Ionian Revolt (499-494 B.C.E.), although ultimately unsuccessful, helped strengthen the Greeks' resolve against a fate of domination by Persia. At the urging of Themistocles, who would later serve as one of the generals at Marathon, the Athenians began to fortify the port of Piraeus and increase the size of their navy. They realized that freedom and independence from Persia could not be achieved without a strong defensive force.

From the Persian perspective, rebellion was intolerable, and the offending Eretrians and Athenians would have to be punished. In addition, Darius hoped to subdue the Cycladic islands and eventually gain control of the Greek mainland, without which his power in the region might not be secure. He reasoned that a successful campaign would teach the Greeks that resistance was futile. A fleet of 600 ships was assembled for the mission. In command were a Mede named Datis and Artaphernes, the king's nephew. Hippias, the exiled Athenian tyrant, accompanied them, no doubt with the hope of regaining power once Athens had been conquered. Their mission was "to reduce Athens and Eretria to slavery" and to bring the captives before the king.

Ambassadors were dispatched to the leading Greek cities to demand "earth and water" as symbols of submission to King Darius. Predictably, Athens and Sparta refused, but most other cities complied.

Datis and Artaphernes headed first to Eretria, conquering many of the Greek islands they passed along the way. Naxos, which had resisted the Persian-supported coup of

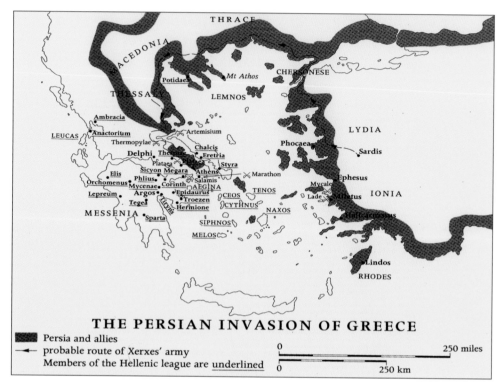

THE PERSIAN INVASION OF GREECE

■ Persia and allies
◄— probable route of Xerxes' army
Members of the Hellenic league are underlined

0 _____ 250 miles

0 _____ 250 km

Darius and his army conquered Thrace in their continuing move toward Greece. In 480-479 B.C.E. Darius's son, King Xerxes I, would continue his father's plans for the invasion of Greece.

Aristagoras received special devastation. When the fleet arrived at Eretria, it met with some hostility, but the Eretrians were not united in their resistance and could hold out for only a week before the city fell to the Persians through the treachery of several aristocrats. In accordance with the orders of Darius, Eretria's temples were burned and its people enslaved.

Things would not be so easy at Athens, and Herodotus, perhaps embellishing his account for the sake of a good story, paints a picture of an overconfident Persian army sailing from Eretria in triumph and anticipating an equally successful engagement with the Athenians. At the urging of Hippias, the fleet landed at Marathon and set up camp while the aged tyrant made contact with conspirators in Athens (perhaps the Alcmaeonids) who might betray the city and join him in power.

There were several good strategic reasons for selecting the bay of Marathon as the landing site. First and foremost, it was undefended, unlike the bay of Phalerum. Second, it was relatively close to the Persians' supply base in Euboea. Finally, the Persian fighting force included cavalry, which could be used to good advantage on the open plain of Marathon. In addition to its strategic benefits, Marathon offered Hippias a good symbolic reason for choosing the site: in 546 his father, Pisistratus, had landed at Marathon before becoming tyrant of Athens. Perhaps Hippias would be able to recapture his father's glory.

Meanwhile, news of the fall of Eretria had reached Athens. Fearing that they could not stand up to the Persians alone, the Athenians appealed to Sparta for aid. At that time, the best way to convey this request was to send a fast long-distance runner. Within four days, Athens had its answer: the Spartans were willing to help out against the Persians, but they were engaged in a solemn festival in honor of the god Apollo and, for religious reasons, were unable to leave Sparta on a military mission until the next full moon. Although the Spartans could not be counted on, help, in the form of 1,000 soldiers, did come from the Plataeans, whom the Athenians had once assisted in their own struggle for independence.

Once the Persians were encamped at Marathon, the Athenian people had to decide whether their army should retain a defensive posture in the city or march out to Marathon and engage the enemy there. The Assembly met to decide the question, and at the urging of Miltiades, a leading general, the citizens voted to send the 9,000-man army to Marathon. By the morning of September 11, 490 B.C.E., the Athenian soldiers had pitched camp at the southern end of the plain of Marathon, and by the end of the day they were joined by the Plataeans. The first major battle of the Greco-Persian wars would soon be at hand.

The Ionian Revolt and the events that followed it raise a series of historical "what if?" questions. If Megabates, the Persian admiral, had not tipped off the Naxians of his upcoming invasion, would an undefended Naxos have fallen? If it fell, it is unlikely that Aristagoras would have had any motive to instigate revolution. Would the Ionians have risen up anyway, or might they have given in after witnessing defeat at the hands of a stronger power? And if the Ionian Revolt had not happened, or if the Athenians had not participated, would Persia have sought to attack Athens at Marathon, and, if so, would Athens have had the resolve to win?

J. B. Bury, one of the foremost Greek historians of the 20th century, offers an insightful perspective: "The Persian invasion was brought about by the same political causes which enabled Athens to withstand it. The Ionian Greeks would not have risen in revolt but for the growth of a strong sentiment against tyrannies—the same cause which over-threw the Pisistratids and created Marathonian Athens."

To put it another way, democracy was taking root in Greece at the same time that the Persian Empire was expanding westward. To maintain control over distant lands, the Persians needed the help of local tyrants who would run puppet governments loyal to the king in Susa. When the local tyrants found their authority challenged by democratic impulses, Persia had little choice but to assert its might in an effort to keep the empire intact. The trouble was that the same democratic impulses that rejected tyranny were also prepared to reject an empire. The stage was set for a massive conflict, not just of might, but also of will and ideas, of democracy against autocracy, of west against east, of Greece against Persia.

As Bury's analysis implies, the movement of history is seldom dependent on single events but rather on broader trends that help guide events to develop as they do. Still, if there was ever a day when a single event made a difference, when things really could have gone either way, and when the participants believed—even at the time—that one day helped shape the destiny of a people, it was the 17th day of the lunar month Boedromion (September 19) in the year 490 B.C.E.: the day of the Battle of Marathon.

This relief from the palace of King Darius shows him sitting on his throne. He ruled Persia from 521 to 486 B.C.E.

The Generals

Tell me now, you Muses who have your homes on Olympus,
For you, who are goddesses, are there, and you know all things,
And we have heard only the rumor of it and know nothing.
Who then of those were the chief men and lords of the Danaans?

So begins the famous catalogue of ships in Book 2 of Homer's *Iliad,* a poem whose words teach that to understand a war, it is necessary to know something of the men who fought it: their backgrounds and motivations, their character and personal skills. This chapter discusses the generals and the next chapter continues with the rank-and-file soldiers.

The Greeks

Of all the generals at Marathon, none was more influential than Miltiades. He was born in Athens in the year 550 B.C.E. and claimed to be descended from Aeacus, a son of Zeus, but his mortal family was actually quite distinguished. His father, Cimon, was a member of the influential Philiad clan; however, after he had a falling out with the Athenian tyrant Pisistratus, son of Hippocrates, he was forced into exile. During this period, he earned the honor of victory in the four-horse chariot race at Olympia. During the next Olympics, he competed again with the same team of horses and again finished first, but, as Herodotus reports,

> he allowed Pisistratus to be declared the winner—an action which reconciled him to Pisistratus and so enabled him to return to Athens under a truce. The same team of horses gained him victory at a subsequent Olympic Games, but then, as it happened, he was killed by Pisistratus' sons. . . . Cimon is buried outside Athens, on the far side of a road called "through Coele." The mares which won him three victories at Olympia are buried opposite him.

Cimon's half-brother, also called Miltiades, was a military leader of some significance. He brought the island of Lemnos under Athenian control, and earlier in his career, he had led a band of Athenian colonists to the Thracian Chersonesus, known today as the Gallipoli peninsula in modern Turkey. After his death, the younger Miltiades, who had proven his administrative skills as archon of Athens in 524, would assume leadership of this colony. Control over the Chersonesus was of great strategic importance to the Athenians, whose grain imports required safe passage across the Black Sea, and Miltiades solidified his ties to the region in 515 when he married Hegisipyle, the daughter of Olorus, King of Thrace.

In 513 B.C.E. the Persian king Darius marched his army into Europe to wage war on the Scythians. After building a bridge over the River Ister, the king left a detachment of Ionian and Aeolian Greeks to guard the bridge against the Scythians, who might try to destroy it and thereby cut off the Persians' return home. Among the Greeks leaders was Cimon's son Miltiades. When the Scythians arrived at the bridge, they proposed to the Ionians that their two peoples should join forces against the Persians and ultimately free the Greeks from Persian imperial control. Miltiades was in favor of the proposal and advocated the destruction of the bridge, but Hisitaeus of Milteus was able to persuade the other Ionian commanders to remain loyal to Darius. Having taken a position against Darius, Miltiades felt compelled to flee and give up control of the Chersonesus, but the Roman biographer Nepos would later remark that the general was nonetheless deserving of high praise because he was more interested in public freedom than in maintaining his own power. When it came time to face the armies of Darius at Marathon, there was no doubt that Miltiades should be among the commanders.

Two years after the encounter with the Scythians, Miltiades had a scuffle with the Phoenicians, allies of the Persians. The Phoenicians, he ascertained, were headed for the Chersonesus and had already reached Tenedos, an island near Troy, off the modern Turkish coast. Fearing reprisals from the Persian king, Miltiades loaded up five ships and set sail for Athens. En route, he encountered the Phoenician fleet, which attacked and captured one of his ships—the one commanded by

Metiochus, his eldest son. The Phoenicians thought they has won a great prize and eagerly surrendered Metiochus to Darius, who, much to their surprise, lavished the son of Miltiades with gifts and a Persian wife. These events provide an important insight into the personality and strategic mindset of Darius, who often sought to bring the Greeks under Persian control as much by patronage and diplomacy as by force.

There can be little doubt of Miltiades's skill at Marathon. He had to manage competing political forces, forge an alliance of generals willing to engage the Persians, select the time and place for the engagement, and devise a winning battle plan despite being massively outnumbered. The fact that the Greeks sustained relatively few casualties is a testimony to the general's skill.

Success at Marathon led to a subsequent command at Paros, where Miltiades led a fleet of 70 ships against the Parians, who had previously given aid and comfort to the Persians. The general was on the verge of capturing the town when a brush fire arose one night in a distant grove. In time the flames grew visible at Paros where they were interpreted as a sign from the fleet of Darius that Persian aid was on the way. As a result, the Parians decided not to surrender, and Miltiades decided to retreat. It is unclear why Miltiades retreated, for his actions at Paros were not consistent with his actions at Marathon. He may have believed that his army could not fend off both the Parians in front and the Persians from the rear, especially if Darius had sent a massive force to exact revenge for Marathon. Or perhaps he felt that his current mission of retribution was not worth the same level of risk as a battle fought to defend against an invader. Whatever his reasons, the people of Athens were angered by his decision and quickly accused him of treason. Unable to defend himself because of wounds he received during the siege of Paros, Miltiades was convicted and fined 500 talents, a sum he could not pay. He was immediately thrown into prison.

The Roman biographer Nepos reports that Miltiades was a man of such great kindness and so remarkably obliging that he would never refuse to meet with anyone who desired to speak with him, no matter how humble of birth. "He had great influence with all the Greek states, a famous name, and a great reputation as a soldier." Nevertheless, the people of Athens were so afraid of Persian conquest that, since they were uncertain about Miltiades's actions, it seemed better to condemn an innocent man than to free one who might be guilty. Thus, the glorious victor of Marathon would die in prison as a broken man in 489 B.C.E.

Of all the associates of Miltiades at Marathon, none was more famous than Themistocles. Born in the 520s B.C.E., Themistocles was the son of the Athenian nobleman Neocles, who disinherited his son for living recklessly and squandering the family estate. According to Nepos, however, "this affront, instead of breaking his spirit, aroused his ambition." From an early age, he took an active role in public affairs and soon became famous both for his skill at speaking in the Assembly and for his ability to implement the programs it passed.

His first major military command came in the war against Corcyra. He persuaded the people of Athens to use some of the revenues from the silver mines at Laurium for the construction of a massive navy, which he then used to defeat the Corcyrans and keep pirates in check.

These victories, coupled with his success at Marathon, earned Themistocles the command of Greek forces at Thermopylae and Salamis, the post-Marathon battles that ultimately removed the Persian threat against Greece for good. According to most modern historians, these battles,

The Athenian statesman and naval commander Themistocles realized that Greece needed a powerful navy to fight the Persians.

which will be discussed in chapter 6, would not have been successful had it not been for the foresight of Themistocles in establishing a powerful navy.

The political career of Themistocles was no less important than his military endeavors. A patron of the arts, Themistocles produced at least one tragic play, supplying the funds for the chorus from his own personal resources.

He also understood that victory in war depended, in part, on popular support, and Themistocles cultivated that support by implementing reforms that gave people a greater personal stake in the democracy they would be called to defend. One of his most significant reforms was the practice of ostracism, which is the public banishment of a citizen chosen by popular vote. The exiled individual would retain his property and rights of citizenship, but his expulsion was thought to cleanse the city (both symbolically and literally) by removing a troublesome person. Each year the Assembly would vote whether or not to hold an ostracism in the first place, and if it was approved, a second ballot would select the person to be exiled.

Aristides was a wealthy Athenian who became archon shortly after the Battle of Marathon. As a leader, he had a reputation for fairness and honesty and earned the nickname "Aristides the Just." A famous anecdote was widely circulated in antiquity to illustrate his character. One year the Assembly voted to hold an ostracism. To choose the person who would be exiled, each citizen would inscribe a shard of pottery with the name of the person he believed should be ostracized. The man with the most votes was then sent into exile. During the voting for this ostracism, Aristides is said to have assisted an illiterate man who was turned away from participating because he could not write. When asked whom he intended to vote for, the man replied that he wanted to banish Aristides because he was tired of hearing everybody call him "The Just," whereupon Aristides wrote his own name upon the shard.

Like Themistocles, Aristides played a crucial role in defeating the Persians not only at Marathon but also in the battles that followed. He was instrumental in establishing the Confederacy of Delos in 477 B.C.E. Sometimes called the "Delian League," the confederacy was a military alliance to which member city-states would contribute ships and/or

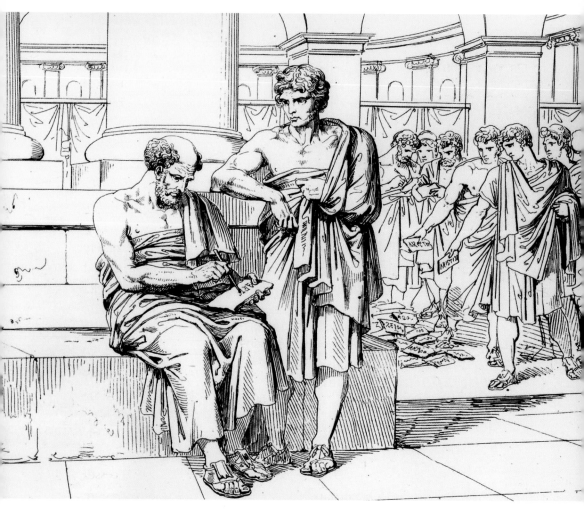

Aristides was a Greek general at the Battle of Marathon. He is shown writing his name on a piece of pottery as part of an ostracism proceedings.

money to support the building and operation of a massive fleet. Its primary mission was to defend Greece against Persian invasion, and it was run by a representative council that met on the island of Delos. Although Aristides took pains to ensure the equitable distribution of resources and responsibilities, Themistocles, his fellow Athenian and sometime rival, saw to it that Athens retained effective control of the league.

Little is known about Callimachus of Aphidnae. He served as the *polemarch,* or War Archon, of Athens in 490. The details of his conduct at the Battle of Marathon will be discussed in chapter 5. Herodotus makes it seem as if Miltiades was the true mastermind of the whole operation, but many modern historians suspect that Callimachus took a more active role than has been reported. Indeed, the polemarch should have had the overall command of the mission under the laws that were in effect at the time of the battle.

The Persians

On the Persian side, King Darius was the man ultimately responsible for the conduct of the war. Darius I, called "Darayavaush" in his native Persian, was born in 521 B.C.E.. An ambitious man, he first rose to prominence as one of the seven nobles who put down the rebellion against Cambyses led by a man posing as his brother Smerdis (see chapter 1). Since there was no legitimate successor, a new king had to be chosen, and it was decided that the man whose horse neighed first before sunrise would be made king. With a little help from the keeper of his stables, Darius arranged to have his horse neigh first and was therefore declared the sovereign.

Darius was a capable leader with many military successes to his credit. Of perhaps greater significance, however, were his political and financial reforms, which strengthened the administration of the empire. An ancient inscription bears witness to his accomplishments:

> I am Darius the Great King, King of Kings, King of many countries, son of Hystaspes, descendant of Achaemenes. Says Darius the King: "By the favor of Ahuramazda [the Persians' chief god], these are the countries which I got into my possession with the help of the Persian folk, countries which felt fear of me and bore me tribute: Elam, Media, Babylonia,

Arabia, Assyria, Egypt, Armenia, Cappadocia, Sardis, Ionians who are of the mainland and those who are by the sea, and countries which are across the sea, Sagartia, Parthia, Drangiana, Aria, Bactria, Sogdiana, Chorasmia, Sattagydia, Arachosia, Sind, Gandara, Scythians, Maka." Says Darius the King, "If thus you shall think, 'May I not fear fear of any other,' protect the Persian people; if the Persian people shall be protected, thereafter for the longest time unbroken happiness will come down from Ahura upon the royal house.

Darius appointed Datis and Artaphernes to lead the campaign against Athens and Eretria in 490. Datis was in many ways a logical choice, for he was successful against the Greeks during the Ionian Revolt of the 490s. Although few details of his life and career beyond the Battle of Marathon have survived, Herodotus does report one anecdote that reveals either a sense of religious piety or a talent for propaganda, depending on the interpretation. When Datis was seen approaching Delos, the sacred island of Apollo and Artemis, during the Ionian Revolt, the Delians fled in fear. Datis immediately ordered his fleet to sail off to a different island while he sought out the Delians. Once he ascertained their location, he sent the following message: "Reverend gentlemen, why have you run away? You have a mistaken impression of me. Even if it were not for the king's instructions, I would certainly have enough sense, faced with the birthplace of two gods, not to inflict the slightest harm on the land itself or its inhabitants. So why don't you return and come back to live in Delos?"

Herodotus says, "This was the message Datis delivered to the Delians. He then heaped up three hundred talents of frankincense on the altar and burned it as an offering."

Artaphernes, the commander at Marathon, was the son

A staircase relief from the audience hall of King Darius shows a procession of tribute bearers from the countries of Lydia, Scythia, Bactria, and Cilicia.

of Artaphernes, the half-brother of King Darius—a relationship that likely played a role in securing his military position. The elder Artaphernes was involved in the Scythian campaign of 513 in which Miltiades had been involved. He was later appointed governor of Sardis and successfully defended the city against Greek attacks during the Ionian Revolt. His son Artaphernes, called "Vindafarnah" in Persian, was therefore motivated to lead a campaign designed to punish those states that had supported the rebellious Ionians.

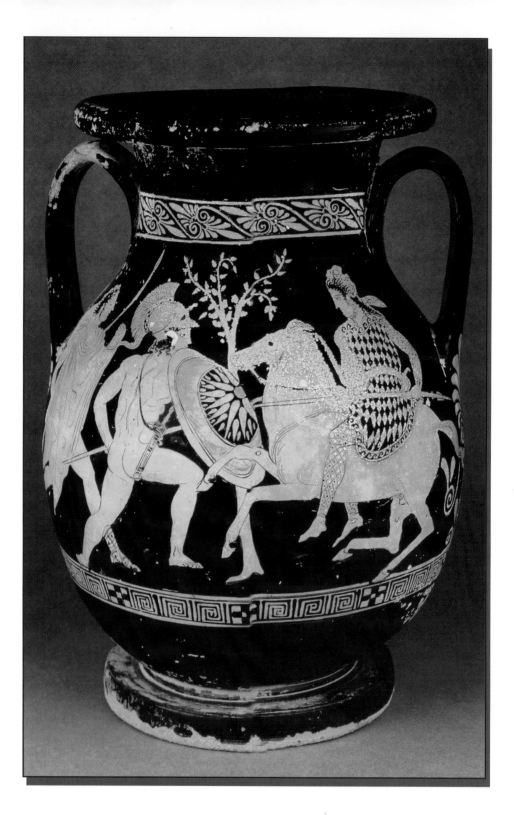

Fighting between a cavalryman and a Greek infantryman is depicted on this Greek vase. Many of these Persian horsemen were at the Battle of Marathon.

The Soldiers

O nly sketchy details are known about the lives of the generals at Marathon. Information about the individual soldiers who fought and died that day is practically nonexistent. Historians of modern wars can interview living veterans and collect and study soldiers' letters. Indeed, the personal stories of individual combatants have become an integral part of modern military historical writing. No such documents exist for ancient wars, and while Herodotus did interview some of the veterans of Marathon, his narrative concentrates on the leaders of the war and the actions of the army as a whole rather than the exploits of particular soldiers. Occasionally, the fate of a regular soldier is revealed, as when "Cynegeirus the son of Euphorion was grabbing hold of the stern of one of the ships [and] was fatally wounded when his hand was chopped off by a battle-ax." In this case, however, the fame of Cynegeirus's family or the colorful nature of the story is probably what motivated Herodotus to include it.

Although little is known about individuals, it is nevertheless possible to get a fairly good sense of the types of people who fought on the side of the Greeks. The front line of soldiers consisted of *hoplites,* or heavily armed infantrymen. Because a Greek soldier had to supply his own armaments, these *pandemei*, or "best armed men," were landowners of significant means who perhaps had a special financial stake in preserving their estates and way of life. The cost of supplying arms also meant that many hoplites were well established in life, and therefore middle-aged rather than young men. Most were farmers who worked their own land—vineyards, orchards, fields of grain—alongside paid laborers. Lightly armed soldiers of more modest means filled out the ranks.

When Greeks fought against Greeks, mostly over land, battles were more about pushing the enemy back to gain some ground than actually killing men. At Marathon, however, where the Greeks were fighting a foreign invader, combat was a brutal and bloody business. The clash of bronze arms and iron swords and the sounds of screaming men must have been both deafening and terrifying. Blood flew everywhere as flesh was pierced and limbs cut off. Dust and sweat mixed with blood on the soldiers' faces, sometimes making it hard to see.

While Herodotus omits the details of the carnage at Marathon, Xenophon, another ancient historian, provides a vivid description of the scene after a similar battle: "The earth was stained with blood, and the remains of friends and enemies lay side-by-side. There were shattered shields, broken spears, and unsheathed swords, some lying about on the ground, others struck in corpses, and others still gripped as if to strike even in death."

Greek War Armor

The standard armor of a typical hoplite consisted of the following: a bronze helmet, often with a plume on top; a bronze breastplate; heavy leather flaps extending from the bottom of the breastplate over the midriff and groin, which offered protection while preserving mobility; greaves, often of bronze, which covered the area from the knee to the ankle; and a large, circular shield. All of the armaments were specially forged to offer maximum protection, and advances in metalworking prior to Marathon gave the Greeks a tremendous defensive advantage. The shield was in many respects a soldier's most important piece of defensive equipment. It was quite large, about 20 pounds, and strapped onto the left arm. Concave in shape, the shield had a lip around the edge that enabled it to rest against the hoplite's left shoulder, a position that could relieve some of the weight during a long battle. Its diameter also needed to be great enough that the shield could cover his torso, left side, and the right side of the soldier next to him, whose right arm was unprotected by his own shield. Collectively, the hoplites formed a *phalanx,* a nearly impenetrable battle line of interlocked shields.

Why would free men willingly submit themselves to such horrors? At the most basic level, the Greek soldiers at Marathon simply fought to defend their homeland against foreign domination. Furthermore, a Greek citizen felt he had a duty—indeed, a moral obligation—to serve his city. In the minds of most Athenians, the rights, freedoms, and opportunities of democracy came with certain responsibilities, and the first among them was military service. At a more fundamental level, however, there was also a sense that war was a matter of honor. The Greek philosopher Plato wrote that war "always exists by nature among all the Greek city-states." Of all human endeavors, war was what revealed character best: to fight and fight well was a way of showing personal virtue and winning honor.

The Persian army consisted of professional soldiers, aristocrats, cavalry, and foreign draftees and allies. Soldiers are depicted here with their shields and spears.

Information about individual soldiers fighting at Marathon is even harder to find for the Persians than it is for the Greeks. In general terms, however, Persian forces differed from their Greek counterparts in two significant ways: the composition of the army and the equipment used.

While the Greek citizen-soldiers were mostly farmers by trade, the heart of the Persian army consisted of professional soldiers who were formally trained, experienced fighters in service of and supported by the Persian king. They were accompanied by various nobles and aristocrats and a large group of foreign soldiers drafted into service during previous Persian conquests. These draftees lacked the motivation of their professional counterparts as well as the motivation to fight to the death. Soldiers of allied states made up the balance of the infantry. The pride of the Persian army was the cavalry, perhaps 5,000 strong at Marathon although it seems that only a small percentage of these knights were actually involved in the fighting.

Persian foot soldiers were trained as highly skilled archers, but they were not very well equipped for hand-to-hand combat with the heavily armed Greek hoplites. Most of the Persians wore relatively soft clothing and used wicker shields, but a few who could afford it strapped metal plates underneath their tunics. The cavalrymen were similarly attired. An illustration of the relative rarity of Persian armor is offered by Herodotus in his account of the Battle of Plataea. Masistius, one of the Persian generals and a skilled horseman, was knocked to the ground when his horse was wounded. Herodotus reported:

> As soon as Masistius landed on the ground the Athenians sprang forward, seized the horse and killed Masistius, although he fought back. At first, in fact, they failed to kill him: next to his skin he was wearing a breastplate made of gold scales, with a red tunic on top, so the Athenians' blows kept hitting the breastplate and achieving nothing. Eventually, however, one of them realized what was happening and struck Masistius in the eye. Only then did he fall to the ground and die.

The Greeks had superior arms as well as a more compelling motivation to fight. The Persians, however, had superior numbers, professional fighters, and a large, highly mobile cavalry. The Greeks seemed, therefore, to be at something of a disadvantage, and it would take a combination of strong leadership, smart planning, determination, and good fortune if they were to have any chance of prevailing in battle.

Heavily armed Greek infantrymen, or hoplites, are shown here ready for battle.

Victory at Marathon

On the night of September 11, 490 B.C.E., the Persians sent out a scouting party to ascertain the Athenian position, and on the 12th, Datis and Artaphernes advanced their troops on the plain of Marathon to a spot some two to three miles from the Greek camp. It remains a matter of speculation why the Persian commanders made this move, but it is plausible to suppose that they had heard of the Spartans' pledge of support and hoped to engage the Greek forces before the aid arrived.

The next move belonged to the Greek generals, who were evenly divided as to their best course of action. Five of the 10 advocated avoiding battle entirely because they feared that the Persians' superior numbers would ensure defeat. Miltiades and

the four remaining generals were in favor of engagement. Since military decisions were made not by a single
commander but by the 10 generals acting collectively, the
deadlock was paralyzing, and Herodotus reports that
"the more cowardly view was beginning to gain the
upper hand."

Miltiades had a solution. Also present in camp was
Callimachus of Aphidnae, the polemarch, or War
Archon, who served as the ceremonial commander in
chief and religious leader of the campaign. In earlier
times, the polemarch had voting rights in military
matters, and the generals agreed that he should cast the
tiebreaking vote. Miltiades was sent to find Callimachus
and escort him to the War Council. On his way, the
general successfully persuaded the polemarch to side
with those who favored combat.

The precise words that Miltiades used to win over
Callimachus are unknown (for nobody else was present
to record the conversation). Herodotus creatively recon-
structs the type of speech the general might have given:

> The future of Athens lies in your hands now,
> Callimachus. You can either cast us down into
> slavery or win us our freedom—and thereby
> ensure that you will be remembered as long as
> there are people alive on this earth, with a
> higher reputation even than Harmodius and
> Aristogiton. Athens' position is more precarious
> now than it ever has been before, throughout its
> history. There are two alternatives: submission
> to the Persians—and we have seen what will
> happen if we fall into Hippias' hands—or
> victory, in which case we might well become the
> leading city in Greece. How could that happen,
> you ask? And why is it up to *you* to determine the

course of events? I will explain. The ten generals are evenly divided between those who want to engage the enemy, and those who are advising against it. Failure to take the enemy on will, I'm sure, generate serious civil war, and in the upheaval the Athenians will be disposed to collaborate with the Persians. However, if we engage the enemy before this or any other unsound view infects the minds of some Athenians, and if the gods are impartial, we can get the better of the Persians in the battle. So it is entirely up to you now; it all depends on you. If you support my point of view, your country will be free and your city will become the leader of Greece. But if you side with those who are disinclined to fight, your reward will be the opposite of these benefits."

Miltiades's words achieved their goal, and Callimachus voted to engage the Persians, but a practical problem remained for the Greeks. Day-to-day operational command of the army fell to single generals on a rotating basis. The four men who had sided with Miltiades freely surrendered their turns at command to him, but the five dissenters could not be counted on to follow suit or act decisively at a time of crisis. In this instance, however, luck favored Athens, for command fell to Miltiades at all the crucial moments.

By September 12, then, the Greeks had resolved to engage the enemy and aligned their troops to face the Persians on the plain of Marathon. According to custom, the polemarch Callimachus took up position with his division on the right wing, which was situated at the border of the Little Marsh in order to protect it from being outflanked, or attacked from the side, by the

Marion Carnegie Library
206 S. Market St
Marion, IL 62959

Persian army. The 10 generals spaced their troops out along the line in a predetermined order of divisions that placed the celebrated generals Themistocles and Aristeides at the very center. The Plataeans occupied the left wing. To guard against outflanking from this side, the Greeks constructed an *abatis,* or defensive obstacle of trees that had been cut down and their branches hewn and sharpened for added protection against the Persian cavalry.

A Greek phalanx, or battle line, was typically eight rows deep and consisted of hoplites, or heavily armed infantrymen, spaced about a yard apart, their shields interlocked to form a solid front that was very difficult to penetrate. It is reasonable to assume that the hoplites were arranged in this fashion when they took their initial positions on the line, which would have extended about 3,750 feet (or about 7/10 of a mile) given the number of troops.

For six days, the two sides faced each other, and each night the Greek phalanx inched slowly forward until the opposing armies were eight stades, or about 4,850 feet apart, just under a mile. The Spartan army had not yet left its homeland, and the conspirators in Athens had not yet signaled the Persians. It was the night of September 18, and Miltiades was in command.

Each side was looking for some opportunity or advantage, and this night fortune was on the side of the Greeks: The Persian cavalry had become separated from its infantry. The precise reasons for this separation continue to be debated by modern historians. According to one theory, they had already left or were preparing to leave with Datis and some other troops on a mission to attack Athens itself. A more widely held view is that the horses were simply grazing at a spring on the far side of the Great Marsh and that their caretakers misjudged the

This diagram illustrates a phalanx of Greek soldiers. This formation of armed men in eight rows was typical in battles at that time.

timing of the return because, for the first time that month, the moon did not set until after dawn. For whatever reason, the Persian army's greatest threat, its cavalry, would be absent from the fight if the Greeks acted immediately. But how would they know about the horses? Through another bit of good luck, some Ionian troops under the command of Artaphernes and stationed on the right wing of the Persian army crossed over to the Greek side and shouted, "The cavalry are away!" Given that the Ionians were a Greek people living under Persian rule and considering that they were almost certainly drafted into service, such "treachery" was not entirely without motivation.

Despite these favorable developments, the Greeks remained at a disadvantage, for they were severely out-numbered by the Persians. A carefully conceived strategy and flawless execution would still be required to win the battle. The Greeks were especially vulnerable on their left wing, not because of any inferiority on the part of the Plataeans but because the Persian line extended at least 200 yards farther to the west. To prevent being out-flanked, Miltiades extended the Greek line to match the breadth of the Persian formation and added to his abatis. If close spacing was to be maintained in the front ranks, the general would have to sacrifice depth.

Knowing the habits of an opponent is crucial to military success, and Miltiades correctly anticipated that the Persian commanders would concentrate their best talent in the center of the line and place less experienced fighters on the wings. Some generals might have coun-tered with an equally fortified center on the Greek side, but Miltiades chose a different course: he thinned out the center to a depth of four or perhaps even three rows and built up the wings. His strategy was to accept a calculated (and hopefully limited) loss in the center, win overwhelmingly on the sides, and then have his wing divisions turn in on the elite Persian center, effectively cutting it off from the routed Persian flanks. It seemed like a logical gamble, but only the actual course of battle would tell if the choice was a wise one.

It was now dawn on September 19, 490 B.C.E. As the

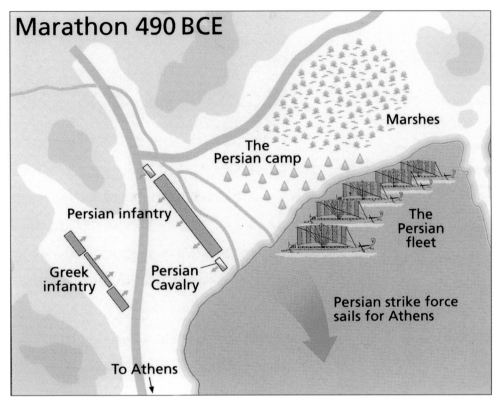

Marathon 490 BCE

Marshes

The Persian camp

Persian infantry

The Persian fleet

Greek infantry

Persian Cavalry

Persian strike force sails for Athens

To Athens

During the Battle of Marathon, the Greeks were able to push the Persian line to the marshes, where many soldiers perished. At the same time, the Persian navy sailed to Athens to continue the fighting.

sun rose over the bay, its rays flickering on the surface of the water and on the bronze armor of the Greeks, a palpable nervous energy must have been felt on the plain of Marathon. As was their custom before a fight, the Greeks made a sacrifice to their gods and consulted the chief priests to confirm that the omens were favorable for battle. When these obligations were discharged, Miltiades reportedly raised his right arm, pointed in the direction of the Persian line, and gave the command, "Charge at them!" The phalanx moved forward as rapidly as possible while still maintaining a tight formation. When the hoplites came within range of the Persian archers at a distance of about 150 yards, they probably broke into a full-scale run. Herodotus describes the encounter this way:

> When the Persians saw the Athenians running towards them, they got ready to receive them, but they thought the Athenians must be mad—mad enough to bring about their utter destruction—because they could see how few of them there were, and that their charge was unsupported by cavalry or archers. That was the invaders' assessment of the situation, but when the Athenians came to grips with them all along the line, they fought remarkably well. They were the first Greeks known to charge enemy forces at a run, and the first to endure Persian dress and the men wearing it.

The veterans interviewed by Herodotus reported a long battle. Modern scholars estimate a duration of about an hour for the initial conflict and another two for the skirmishes that followed. As Miltiades had predicted, his densely packed wings got the better of their Persian counterparts, who were eventually compelled to retreat. In the center, however, the Persians and their allies, the Sacae, had the upper hand, and it was probably here that they inflicted the most casualties as they drove the Greek line back toward its camp. At this point, the strategy of Miltiades came into play. With the Persian flanks dispersed and in retreat, the Greek and Plataean wings rotated into what might have been a double pincer formation. The difficulty in executing this complex rotation on such a large scale should not be underestimated, but the hoplites were well trained and well commanded. Just as the Greek wings prepared to engage the driving Persian center, the Persian

Marathon: An Ancient Victory and a Modern Foot Race

When the Persian camp had been captured and it was clear that the Greeks had won the battle of Marathon, a runner was dispatched to Athens with the news of the victory.

In 1896, when the first modern Olympics were held in Athens, the "marathon" race was instituted as a commemoration of the ancient Athenian triumph and the messenger's famous victory run. The length of the race was fixed at 26.2 miles, the distance from the modern town of Marathona to Athens. Historians recognize, however, that the battle was fought not in the town but in the plain of Marathon, suggesting a slightly shorter distance to Athens. Unfortunately, there is no way of knowing from what precise point the runner was dispatched. If he departed from the Greek camp, as is likely, a distance of 24 miles comes closer to the truth. If he were sent from the field or from the captured Persian camp, he would have had a slightly longer run.

Either way, the real prize for endurance goes not to the Marathon runner but to the courier sent on foot from Athens to Sparta in order to ask for aid before the battle. His name is variously given as Philippides or Phidippides, and he covered a distance of 140 miles within two days and then had to run all the way back to Athens with the Spartans' reply—a total of 280 miles in four days. Some historians would like to think that Philippides was given the honor of carrying the news of victory at Marathon back to Athens, but the ancient sources offer conflicting information about this hypothesis.

cavalry finally appeared and probably had some success against the wings, but the horsemen had arrived too late and were ultimately ineffective in the close quarters of hand-to-hand combat. The Persians and Sacae recognized their predicament and fled, and the Greeks pursued them toward the Great Marsh. Despite Persian attempts to cover their retreat, the Greeks were nevertheless able to drive many of their adversaries into the marsh where those who could not swim perished by drowning. Meanwhile, another branch of the Persian army headed for the coast where the Greeks engaged them in a battle for the ships. Once again, Herodotus offers a vivid description:

> During this melee the War Archon was killed, fighting bravely, and one of the commanders, Stesilaus the son of Thrasylaus, died as well. It was also at this point that while Cynegeirus the son of Euphorion was grabbing hold of the stern of one of the ships he was fatally wounded when his hand was chopped off by a battle-ax. A number of other famous Athenians fell as well. The Athenians captured seven of the Persian ships in this way, but the invaders managed to put to sea with the rest of their fleet.

At this point, the Persians might have headed for home, but there was treachery afoot in Athens where conspirators were planning to open the gates to the invading Persians in the absence of the Athenian army. A signal was flashed, probably from Mt. Pentelicus or Mt. Agrilika, at about 9:00 A.M., some three hours after the initial hostilities. The Persians sent a detachment to pick up the Eretrian prisoners while the main fleet turned south, aided by a strong northeasterly wind. The Greeks would have to hurry back to Athens on foot or the city would be lost. Time was truly of the essence, especially if, as some scholars believe, Datis had already left with a detachment of soldiers and the bulk of the cavalry early in the morning before the fighting at Marathon had even begun. The only temporal advantage held by the Greeks was the fact that it was faster to get back to Athens by a direct land route than by the combination of sea and land that lay ahead for the Persians: 7 to 8 hours as opposed to 10 to 12. Still, there was not much time to spare.

Aristeides was left behind to guard the Greek camp and the Persian spoils it now contained and to safeguard the bodies of the slain soldiers who would have to be buried. The main force made the 24-mile journey back to Athens, as fast as possible. Modern historian Peter Green eloquently describes the return:

> The reappearance of the Marathon warriors—grim, indomitable, caked with dust and sweat and dried blood—not only gave Datis pause for thought; it also, obviously, came as an unexpected shock to the Alcmaeonids and the pro-Persian party. A lot of people in Athens must have silently switched sides in a hurry: Datis would get no help from within the walls now.

The Persians realized that they had no chance of success and sailed off in disgrace. The Greeks had successfully defended Athens and with remarkably few casualties: 192. By contrast, the Persians lost 6,400 men, if the figure of Herodotus is to be believed.

Construction of the Parthenon began in 497 B.C.E. to celebrate Greek victories over the Persians. The temple was built to honor Athena, the Greek goddess of wisdom, and she was represented by a large gold and ivory statue, as shown in this reconstruction.

The Immediate Aftermath

To have achieved such a resounding victory with so few casualties was a military feat that the Athenians immediately ranked among the greatest achievements of their city. In celebration, they began construction of a new temple on the Acropolis in 497 B.C.E. Subsequent wars with the Persians would prevent its completion, but the site chosen for the temple would be the future home of the Parthenon, a grand temple to Athena built during the Age of Pericles—in part as a consequence of the events that sprang from Marathon.

There were also celebrations at Delphi, site of an important shrine to Apollo and home to the Athenian treasury. To honor the god for assisting them in battle, the Athenians consecrated an addition to the temple where they displayed the spoils of war.

Although Athens could be justly proud of its accomplishments at Marathon, it was not the only, or even the leading, power of the Greek world. The Spartan king Cleomenes stood at the head of the Peloponesian League, to which Athens belonged, and Aegina possessed a much more powerful navy and was sometimes sympathetic to the Persian cause. To deter Aegina from assisting Persia during the years leading up to Marathon, the Athenians convinced Cleomenes to intervene by capturing 10 hostages from Aegina and turning them over to Athens. After Cleomenes died, however, Aegina hoped to persuade the new king to reclaim the hostages. But before the king could give an answer, the Athenians announced that they had no intention of returning the hostages, and in 487 a war broke out. Athens quickly discovered that it would need a strong navy to hold its own against Aegina. Accordingly, it began a build-up of its fleet, which lasted for several years and without which Athens might not have been able to stand up to Persia in the future.

Political changes accompanied such military developments. The Council of Cleisthenes, intended to be one of the central elements of Athenian democracy, found its power growing weaker and weaker as the archons took more and more power for themselves. A new system for appointing archons was put into place to check their power. Instead of having the people elect the archons directly, they were chosen by lot from a large group of previously elected magistrates. Such a "reform" may, in fact, seem antidemocratic to modern sensibilities, but its intent was to make it unlikely that influential politicians would receive the additional power of the archonship. As a consequence, the position of archon was diminished in importance, and the more representative council saw its authority increase.

It is in this climate that Themistocles, one of the 10 generals at Marathon, emerged as perhaps the most important political leader of his age. Having experienced the might of Persia first hand on the plain of Marathon, Themistocles understood that the great eastern empire would not accept defeat without reprisal and therefore remained a serious threat. Furthermore, Aegina's powerful navy posed a threat of its own, especially if it were ever to come into a direct alliance with Persia. The only suitable defense, Themistocles reasoned, would be for Athens to develop an even stronger navy of its own.

As archon in 493/2 B.C.E., Themistocles already began the fortification of the Piraeus, the leading port in Athens. Given the increased importance of the council, the general was still able to exert great influence even after his term as archon had expired. He used his considerable powers of persuasion to win support for the construction of a defensive wall around the harbor. More importantly, however, Themistocles oversaw the construction of a 200-ship navy. While it was certainly true that even with these new ships the Greeks would still be outnumbered by the Persians, at least now they had a fighting chance.

While Athens was reshaping its government and transforming itself into a naval power, Persia was undergoing changes of its own. Darius promptly began preparations for another campaign to avenge those slain at Marathon. When the king died in 486, his successor Xerxes had to put aside the mission temporarily so he could suppress a rebellion in Egypt that demanded immediate attention.

Once Egypt had been brought under control, Xerxes seems to have been undecided about whether or not to proceed against Greece. His cousin Mardonius urged attack, but his uncle Artabanus argued that numerous obstacles stood in the way of success and that any attack would ultimately end in failure. According to Herodotus, a

King Xerxes I of Persia continued with his father's plans to invade Greece. Xerxes gathered a large force of men and ships to attack the Greeks from both land and sea.

dream came to Xerxes that persuaded him to side with his cousin and resume the preparations for war that Darius had already begun.

Xerxes concluded that his only chance of defeating the newly invigorated Greeks would be to mount an attack from both land and sea. For the army and navy to travel together along the coast of Thrace, it was necessary to dig a one and one-half mile canal along the isthmus of Mount Athos. This task he completed in 483.

In the fall of 481, Xerxes traveled from Susa to Sardis, and there he began to assemble his forces. In 480 the troops were preparing to cross the Hellespont when a storm destroyed the two bridges that had been constructed specifically for this purpose. Xerxes was furious and ordered that the engineers who designed the bridge be beheaded. He further insisted that the sea itself should be punished with three hundred lashes for failing to cooperate with the wishes of the king. His men reportedly struck the waves with chains while shouting, "O bitter water, our lord lays this punishment upon you, for having done him wrong, who never did wrong to you. King Xerxes will cross you whether you wish it or not. It is just that no man sacrifices to you, for you are a treacherous and briny river."

The king then enlisted new engineers to rebuild the bridges. They began by lining up two rows of ships of 360 and 314 each and then connected them by cables. Next, Xerxes erected a marble throne on the opposite shore where he sat for two days as he watched his troops cross.

The full Persian army assembled at Doriscus in Thrace in the summer of 480. The catalog of troops offered by Herodotus is one of his most colorfully written passages, as he describes peoples from 46 different cultures making up a force of 1,200 warships, 3,000 smaller vessels, and more than two million men. The numbers are clearly exaggerated, and modern historians estimate a force of about 800 ships and 180,000 men—still an impressive number.

The Greeks, meanwhile, were making preparations of their own in anticipation of a Persian invasion. Because there was no central government uniting all of Greece, the various city-states needed to meet and devise a plan for defending themselves against the Persian attack force. Since many of the Greek states were not on particularly friendly terms with one another, organizing a common defense required much diplomatic and political skill. Athens wanted to lead the coalition, but many states mistrusted the Athenians, so a Spartan commander was chosen instead.

Spies were dispatched to monitor the preparations of the Persians, and the Greek commanders discussed battle strategies. Although Athens had already assembled a significant navy, the city undertook another massive shipbuilding project. They tried to set aside their political feuds, both within Athens and among competing states. To that end, Aristides was recalled from exile to assist in leading the campaign.

The Persian navy suffered a crushing defeat as the Athenian navy led by Themistocles attacked Persian ships.

The Battles of Thermopylae, Salamis, and Plataea

Faced with an imminent Persian invasion, the Greeks needed to decide upon a first point of defense. At the urging of the Thessalians, they settled on Tempe and sent out 10,000 hoplites, but when the troops arrived, they immediately discovered that there were three different passes through which the Persians might come, and the hoplites could not possibly defend them all effectively. Instead the Greek commanders chose Thermopylae, a narrow mountain pass at the foot of Mt. Oeta on the Malian Gulf, as a suitable alternative, and the Spartan leader Leonidas set out with a force of 7,000 men. He discovered that Thermopylae, too, had a second pass that need to be guarded, but its steep and rugged terrain gave an advantage to the defenders. Furthermore, the fleet,

65

now 271 strong, could take up positions off the coast of Euboea and the entrance to the gulf in an effort to cut off Persian naval support for the attack.

For all their preparations, however, the Greeks seemed to lack confidence that Thermopylae would hold. Although Herodotus reports little apprehension, archaeologists have discovered an inscription bearing a decree by Themistocles that provided for the evacuation of Attica if Thermopylae should fall.

As at Marathon, numbers favored the Persians, but at Thermopylae the Persian advantage was many times greater. As the enemy fleet approached, the Greeks had a bit of good luck when a storm arose and destroyed a substantial number of Persian ships. Even so, the eastern fleet was still enormous—so large that the ships could not all be moored at the same time but had to arrange themselves eight rows deep along the coast. In an effort to attack from the rear, the Persian commanders sent a detachment of 200 vessels to the far side of Euboea, but a second storm destroyed this entire contingent.

Xerxes set up his army on the Malian plain, hoping that the mere sight of his massive force would scare the Greeks into retreat. It is likely he reasoned that victory, though probable, would also be costly since the terrain gave an advantage to those defending the mountain pass, which only a fraction of the Persian army could approach at any one time.

The Greeks, perhaps encouraged by the fortuitous reduction of the Persian fleet, stood firm. Xerxes waited for four days and attacked on the fifth. At first, the Greeks got the better of the Persians in hand-to-hand combat. Soon, however, Xerxes deployed his "Immortals," an elite group of special forces, to go over the mountain and attack the Greeks from the rear—a plan assisted by the treachery of Epialtes, a Greek who assisted the Persians in finding their way.

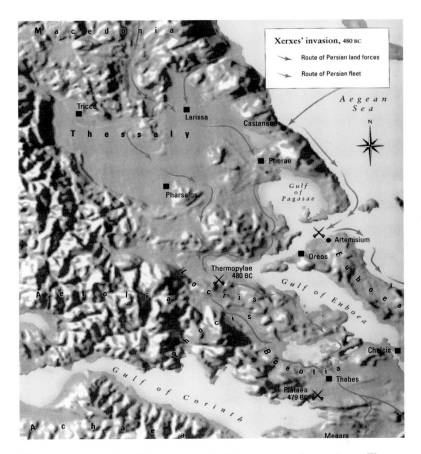

The routes by which Xerxes invaded Greece are shown here. The Greeks defended their territory at Thermopylae but they were defeated, thereby allowing Xerxes to head toward Athens.

When Leonidas heard of the Persian plan, he sent the majority of his force to ambush the Immortals while he remained in the pass with 1,400 men, including his 300 Spartans, who were positioned on the western side. When the Persians approached, Leonidas ordered his men to attack. In the ensuing battle the commander was killed along with all his men. Two brothers of Xerxes also perished. Meanwhile, the Immortals had triumphed over the Greeks in the rear, and they soon made it into the pass. Thermopylae was lost.

This memorial marks the site at the Battle of Thermopylae where Spartan leader Leonidas led Spartan and other Greek forces against the Persians.

Despite the defeat, the legacy of Marathon was very much alive at Thermopylae. Faced with overwhelming odds, the Greeks valiantly stood up against their Persian foes and defended their territory to the death. This defiant attitude is well illustrated by a remark attributed to Dienekes, a Spartan. Upon hearing that the Persians had so many archers that their arrows hid the sun, Dienekes said, "So much the better; we shall fight in the shade." Far from being demoralized by the defeat, the Greeks were inspired by the bravery of those who fought in a hopeless cause. Moreover, the memory of Marathon was still fresh, and the Greeks retained their confidence that victory over the Persians was still possible.

In a political sense, the Spartan sacrifice at Thermopylae was especially important. If there had been any lingering concern that the Spartans had been too slow to help out at Marathon, it was removed at Thermopylae. In addition, their actions toughened the resolve of other city-states, and the Greek alliance grew stronger in the face of a common enemy. The next battle would belong to Greece.

Having triumphed at Thermopylae, Xerxes met little resistance as he marched across Greece toward Athens. Themistocles saw little hope of defending the city, so he ordered a full evacuation. Families packed up their belongings, and the Athenian navy transported the women and children to positions of safety. Each citizen also received a share of the Athenian treasury.

It was decided that a small force ought to be left behind to defend the Acropolis, and the Athenian commanders no doubt hoped that its elevation and steep, rugged slope would provide sufficient natural protection to hold off the Persians. While this evacuation of Athens and limited defense of the Acropolis was almost certainly a calculated risk, a story later arose that an oracle advised the Athenians that all of Attica would be destroyed except for a wooden wall. The majority interpreted this wall to mean the ships, but a few men, convinced that the prophecy referred to a wooden wall protecting the Acropolis, stayed behind.

On or about September 17 of the year 480 B.C.E., Xerxes arrived in Athens and immediately positioned himself to advance on the Acropolis. His archers shot flaming arrows into the wall and burned it down. As the Persian infantry began to ascend the steep slope, the Greeks held them off by rolling stones into their path. This method of defense lasted for about two weeks, but the Persians eventually found an accommodating route up the north slope. Once they reached the summit, there was little hope for the Greeks, who were promptly slain.

Learning of the fall of the Athenian Acropolis, the Greek generals met to devise a strategy. The choice of where to engage the Persians came down to two locations: on the isthmus connecting Attica with the Peloponesus, or Salamis, an island off the western coast of Attica. The council settled on the isthmus, believing that their land forces would be more effective there and that the Peloponesus provided a suitable place for a retreat in case of failure. Themistocles and the Athenians were not happy with this choice, for it meant the effective surrender of their native Attica.

A second council was convened, and Themistocles, anxious to present his arguments, began the debate before he was supposed to. A Corinthian general reportedly admonished the Athenian with the rebuke that "those who stand up too soon in the games are whipped." Without missing a beat, Themistocles retorted, "Yes, but those who start too late are not crowned," and he then proceeded to explain his strategy. Because the Greeks were severely outnumbered, he argued, the Bay of Salamis provided a better strategic location for engaging the Persians. Its close

Greek Military Terms and English Vocabulary

Language is one of the many legacies bequeathed to modern society by ancient Greece. Here are some of the many terms that come from the related spheres of war and politics. The Greek word is given in bold, followed by its literal meaning in parentheses. Related English words follow the colon.

archon (chief magistrate): monarchy, oligarchy

barbaros (foreigner): barbarian

demos (people): demographic, democracy

historia (inquiry): history

hoplites (hoplite): hoplite, a heavily armed foot soldier

phalanx (phalanx): phalanx, a line of tightly packed hoplites

polemos (war): polemic

polis (city-state): politics; police, policy

strategos (general): strategy

quarters would prevent the Greeks from being outflanked and allow only a small portion of the Persian force to fight with them at any given time. Just in case the strategic argument would not be successful in carrying the day, Themistocles added that the Athenian navy, more than half of the total force, would face the Persians only at Salamis and that they would sail off to Italy if any other location were chosen. Not surprisingly, Themistocles got what he wanted.

Herodotus, the chief ancient source about the Persian wars, often enlivens his historical narrative with strange portents that foretell the success (or failure) of the Greek forces. He reports that before the Battle of Salamis, two Greeks saw a great cloud of dust in the distance. They suspected that the cloud had been stirred up by the movements of a vast army, but since they could see no soldiers, they concluded that the dust cloud was a force sent by the gods. One of the men, Dicaeus, offered this explanation:

> The king's forces are going to suffer a major disaster. They can't avoid it. Look, there are no people left in Attica, so this voice is clearly of divine origin, coming from Eleusis to help the Athenians and their allies. If it settles on the Peloponesus, it is Xerxes and his land army that will be in danger; but if it heads toward the Greek ships at Salamis, the king will probably lose his fleet.

When the cloud moved toward Salamis, Dicaeus and his companion became convinced that the Greeks would win a naval victory.

The town of Salamis lies on the eastern side of the island and is protected by a long promontory that stretches eastward into the bay toward a small island called Psyttalea. The Greek fleet took up position behind this promontory, hoping to lure the Persian fleet through the narrow passage and into the bay whose close quarters would be favorable for a Greek attack. The Persians, for their part, favored engagement in the open seas of the Saronic Gulf, where their superior numbers would prove advantageous. Nevertheless, Xerxes massed his ships close to Psyttalea to guard against a Greek attempt to slip off at night. There he was content to wait.

Meanwhile, Themistocles decided that his only chance of success depended on the combination of a careful strategy and a daring deception. He ordered a slave to go to Xerxes and pretend to be an informant for the king. His orders were to say that there was disunity among the Greek commanders—and that part of the message was actually true. However, Themistocles also told the slave to add that the Greek navy planned to attempt an escape that night, and if escape was impossible, the Athenians would turn against their Greek allies and assist the Persians.

Xerxes took the bait and responded exactly as Themistocles hoped: He sent a detachment of 200 Egyptian ships to block the straits of Nisea on the opposite side of the island. If the Greeks actually tried to escape that night, Xerxes thought, then the Egyptian fleet would crush them, and victory would belong to Persia. If they decided not to flee, Xerxes himself would attack in the morning and achieve an easy victory with Athenian aid.

That night, September 19, the Greeks held their positions, and the next morning Xerxes began his attack, which he viewed from a throne erected at the foot of Mount Aegaleos on the mainland. His Ionian detachment sailed between Psyttalea and the island of Salamis while the elite Phoenician squadron took the eastern route between Psyttalea and the mainland. Because the straits were so narrow, the vast ranks of ships had to be reduced to narrow columns of perhaps only three ships traveling abreast.

The Spartans had the responsibility of dealing with the smaller Ionian fleet while the Athenians took on the Phoenicians, attacking them both from the north and on their western flanks as they moved through the narrow passage into the bay. Intense fighting lasted throughout the entire day as the Persians kept filing through the straits, but the Greeks, who were better positioned, kept slaughtering the Persians as they came into view.

Wiser Persian commanders might have reasoned that they could not prevail under such conditions and that it might make more sense to withdraw and reengage the Greeks under more favorable circumstances. Instead, they persisted in the attack in the hope that their superior numbers would eventually wear down the Greek resistance, but Themistocles and his Athenians continued to sink the Persian vessels. As a result, the Persian navy was crushed to such an extent that it not only lost the Battle of Salamis, but also would be unable to inflict much damage later.

A massive land force still remained—one easily capable of defeating the Greeks—but without the navy to keep it supplied, it would not be able to hold out for long. Xerxes made the decision to retreat, but the Persian threat had not yet been permanently removed. A great land victory was needed to complement the naval victory at Salamis, and it would come a year later near a town called Plataea, which stood at the foot of Mount Cithaeron outside of Athens.

If the Athenians under Themistocles had the finest navy in all of Greece, it was the Spartans who boasted the finest infantry. The Greeks began their campaign at the eastern end of Plataea on the road connecting Athens and Thebes. The Spartans held the right wing, and the Athenians were on the left. Greece claimed the first victory when Megarian and Athenian forces routed the troops of Masistius, but they had yet to face the main part of the Persian army.

The two sides skirmished for at least 10 days before the major battle. During this period, the Persian cavalry had much success and eventually cut off the Greeks' water supply. Pausanias, the Greek commander, decided to withdraw a bit at night, but miscommunication and poor execution of orders caused the troops to fall into disarray. Mardonius, the Persian general, seized his opportunity and attacked at dawn.

Caught off guard, the Greeks faltered at first, but the Spartans, traditionally the best trained and best disciplined of the Greek warriors, mobilized and began to drive the Persians back. Mardonius died in this battle, and the valor of the Spartans inspired other troops to action, including the vacillating Athenians, who cut off the Persians on the right side in an effort to prevent reinforcements from assisting in the battle with the Spartans. Now the Persians were in full

The Spartan infantry fought at Plataea and claimed victory along with the Athenians in the battle.

retreat, but the Greeks did not stop until they reached the Persian camp and sacked it. The mighty army of the east had been vanquished, and all of Greece had the Spartans to thank for it because without the bravery and skill of the Spartan hoplites, Plataea almost certainly would have been lost. It is not known whether or not the Greek army would have been able to recover from a loss at Plataea and defeat the Persians elsewhere, but thanks to the Spartans, they did not have to.

Further battles remained in the coming months, but the issue of Persian conquest of Greece had been decided. With the fleet crushed at Salamis and the army routed at Plataea, the Persians had no chance of waging a successful campaign. It took 11 years, but the promise of Marathon was finally fulfilled: one of the world's greatest imperial powers not only could be beaten; it had been.

The Significance
of Marathon

This ancient tomb in Marathon is for the 192 Greek soldiers who died at the Battle of Marathon.

Why does the Battle of Marathon matter? On one level, Marathon is an exciting adventure story full of suspense and intrigue and colorful characters doing daring deeds. For its pure entertainment value, the historical tale of the Battle of Marathon is as compelling as any fiction. But in what sense did the events of 490 B.C.E. make an impact on the people living at the time, and how has this 2,500-year-old battle helped shape the world of today?

To address such questions, it is useful to draw several distinctions because the battle had both short- and long-term effects, physical and psychological ramifications, and political and social consequences. Indeed, the ways in which people responded to the battle were at least as important as the events themselves. The meanings of Marathon were therefore multiple and varied.

The short-term effects of Greek victory should not be underestimated. While it is clear that the battle did not remove the Persian threat for good, it did for the moment save Athens, and perhaps other cities, from destruction and/or slavery. It also bought the Greeks the time they needed to prepare for the future aggressions that almost certainly would have come even if Marathon had been lost. But even if Persia did not yet have designs on the total subjugation of Greece, a strong Persian presence throughout the region certainly would have curtailed freedom—both directly by the Persian lords themselves and indirectly through the local tyrants who received their support from Susa.

The short-term psychological impact was equally profound. To begin, the Greek states had been living in fear of Persian domination and more specifically of reprisals for the Ionian Revolt. Because of Marathon, that fear was at least temporarily removed. Perhaps more important, however, was the confidence that victory gave to the Greeks in general and the Athenians in particular. The Persian army had seemed unstoppable, yet they were stopped on the plain of Marathon. The mere idea that the Persian army was beatable was a thought that few dared to entertain. It is almost impossible to quantify the value of the Greeks' newfound confidence, but there is perhaps something to the famous saying that "nothing succeeds like success." Because they believed that this victory would open the door to others, future victories were more likely to become a reality.

If Marathon held the key to Salamis and Plataea, the battles that ultimately expelled the Persians from Greece

Prisoners of war are shown being auctioned for sale as slaves.

and squelched their imperialist desires, then the implications of those victories must be considered as well. When the Athenians no longer had a foreign enemy to fight, they wisely redirected the vast resources used against Persia toward the internal well-being of the city and its people. While there were still battles to be fought against other enemies, much of the energy that had been directed against Persia was now channeled into more peaceful pursuits, notably politics, philosophy, and the arts.

The independent Greek city-states solidified their alliance with the Confederacy of Delos, whose council was based upon the principle of proportional representation. Athens in particular prospered and helped unify the Greek world under its leadership. The great statesman Pericles strengthened the Athenian democracy by giving more power to all of the citizens and restraining the

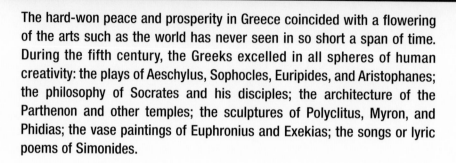

The Growth of Creativity

The hard-won peace and prosperity in Greece coincided with a flowering of the arts such as the world has never seen in so short a span of time. During the fifth century, the Greeks excelled in all spheres of human creativity: the plays of Aeschylus, Sophocles, Euripides, and Aristophanes; the philosophy of Socrates and his disciples; the architecture of the Parthenon and other temples; the sculptures of Polyclitus, Myron, and Phidias; the vase paintings of Euphronius and Exekias; the songs or lyric poems of Simonides.

power of leading aristocratic families. Every citizen had an equal chance of holding public office, while the Assembly and law courts, both controlled by the people themselves, became the most powerful instruments of government. The Athenians put an end to their rivalries with Sparta and Aegina (albeit under terms favorable to Athens), and a formal peace with Persia was struck.

It is almost impossible to know what would have happened if the Greeks had lost the Battle of Marathon, and historians are hesitant to make a large portion of human history dependent upon a single event. Perhaps the Greeks would have recovered from a loss at Marathon and vanquished the Persians anyway. Maybe the democratic impulses sprouting up throughout Greece would have blossomed with just as much energy. Athens might still have emerged as the leading city-state of the Aegean. And perhaps fifth century artists still would have achieved the same heights of glory. But Marathon defined a generation that in turn defined future generations. Without that piece of the puzzle, it is equally possible that Greece would have had a very different fifth century from the one it actually experienced. If so, the modern world would have been changed in many ways.

Indeed, the tangible legacy of ancient Greece influences modern life in countless ways, from politics to the arts to language. If Marathon helped ensure the dominance of the Greek culture to which the Western world is heir, there can be no greater or more pervasive legacy. In addition, as if that were not enough, the meaning of Marathon was, and continues to be, in part, what modern society makes of it: how it translates across the millennia, the lessons learned from it, and the ways in which it inspires people to think and act in response. In the years immediately following the battle, artists offered their own creative responses to the events of September 19, 490 B.C.E, and it is perhaps through their work that the legacy of Marathon finds its fullest expression.

The Battle of Marathon is commemorated in this modern drawing of Greek soldiers attacking Persian ships.

Marathon in Art and Literature

Fifth century Athens was noted for art and literature of the highest sophistication, so it is not surprising that the Battle of Marathon was quick to receive artistic commemoration. Whether through song or story, painting or sculpture, the Athenians used art not only to recall what happened at Marathon and to preserve its memory for future generations, but also to rejoice in their triumph, to inspire their countrymen for future battles, to mourn the slain, and to honor all those who had earned glory in the fight to keep Greece free.

The poet most closely associated with the Battle of Marathon is the tragic playwright Aeschylus, who was born at Eleusis in 525 B.C.E and died in Sicily in 456 or 455. In 490 he fought at

The author of *The Persians*, playwright Aeschylus, depicted here, fought at Marathon and was present for the battles that followed.

Marathon and was at least present 10 years later at Salamis, where he probably was also involved in combat. During the following year, he again fought in the infantry at Plataea.

Aeschylus is the author of ninety plays, only seven of which survive (and one of the seven may be inauthentic). Most of his plays deal with mythological or legendary subjects, but his experiences at Marathon, Salamis, and Plataea may have led him to write *The Persians,* a play about the Persians' reaction to their defeat at Salamis. It is the oldest surviving Greek tragedy and the only one to deal with a historical subject.

Set in the court of Atossa, the mother of Xerxes and widow of Darius, *The Persians* begins with a chorus of elders whose celebration of past victories quickly gives way to anxiety about the fate of the latest campaign. Atossa, plagued by frightening dreams and evil omens, is concerned that the wealth and power of her son will ultimately bring him harm. Eventually, a messenger enters with news of the Battle of Salamis, which is vividly described by the eyewitness poet. Atossa then conjures up the ghost of her husband, who provides a religious explanation for the defeat. At last Xerxes enters and joins the chorus in lamenting his shameful defeat. "Sorrow, Sorrow!" Xerxes cries. "If only I could charm back the souls of brave men as you call the roll of boundless, hateful, unforgettable grief. My heart howls from its bony cage." "Gone, gone, they are dead and gone," the chorus responds as they lead Xerxes home to the music of "slow-dinning dirges."

While Aeschylus is quick to extol the virtues of his victorious Greeks, the play is not merely a piece of pro-Athenian propaganda. The poet treats the vanquished Persians with some sensitivity as he explores the tragic, human consequences of excessive pride and unbridled ambition. Indeed, many modern readers find in *The Persians* a warning for the Athens of the poet's own day, which was building an ever-expanding sphere of influence of its own. If military success can lead to arrogance and arrogance to overreaching, then the Athenians would do well to check their own pride lest it lead to the same tragic consequence faced by Xerxes.

Of all his accomplishments in life, Aeschylus was proudest of his service at Marathon. His epitaph omits all mention of his career as a poet and includes only a single line: "The famous grave of Marathon could tell of his courage and the long-haired Mede knew it well." Indeed, one of the poet's ancient biographers notes that Aeschylus was admired both for his skill as a dramatist and for his character as a man: "All who made their living in the tragic theater went to his tomb to offer sacrifices and recited their plays there. The Athenians liked Aeschylus so much that they voted after his death to award a golden crown to whoever was willing to put on one of his dramas."

Simonides, born in 557 B.C.E, is another poet whose name is closely linked to the Persian wars. In the immediate aftermath of the Battle of Marathon, care for the fallen soldiers was among the first duties of any Greek citizen. Once the bodies had been buried and a tomb established, the Athenians decided to commission an elegy, or poem of lament, for those men who had perished at Marathon. They held a public competition, and Simonides emerged as the winner. Simonides was already a well-respected poet, and one who was especially good at writing emotional dirges, or funeral songs. Aeschylus also entered the competition, but his entry was rejected because "the elegiac meter needs the delicate touch which rouses sympathy, and that, as we have said, is foreign to Aeschylus."

The winning poem of Simonides, unfortunately, has not survived, except for two lines:

> But if it is right, daughter of Zeus, to honor what is best,
> It was the people of Athens who performed it alone.

In addition, Simonides is credited with the authorship of several inscriptions on the base of a monument to veterans of the Persian wars. One seems to refer to Marathon: "These men must have had a stout heart when they took up arms before the gates and checked men eager to burn Athena's glorious seaside city, forcibly turning back the champions of Persia." Another inscription honors the victors at Salamis: "The fame and valor of these men will be undying always, so long as the gods apportion glory to brave men; for both on foot and on swift-sailing ships they kept all Greece from seeing the day of slavery." It is likely that Simonides also provided the inscription for the grave marker at Marathon itself, which is now lost, but the words are preserved by another ancient author: "Fighting to defend the Greeks, the Athenians laid low at Marathon the might of the gold-appareled Medes." Apparently fascinated by the Persian wars, Simonides wrote several full poems about Salamis and Plataea. Even the losing effort at Thermopylae provided inspiration for a poem:

> When men die for their country,
> Fame is their fortune, fair their fate,
> Their tomb an altar; in the place of wailing
> There is remembrance, and their dirge is praise.
> This winding-sheet is such
> As neither mould nor Time that conquers all
> Can fade; this sepulchre
> Of fine men has adopted as its sacristan
> Greece's good name. Witness Leonidas,
> The King of Sparta: he has left
> A monument of valor and perennial fame.

Of the representations of Marathon in ancient art, none is more famous than the Stoa Poikile at the north end of the Athenian Agora, or central marketplace. The Stoa Poikile, or "painted colonnade," was a covered walkway with a solid wall on one side and columns on the other. The wall was adorned with paintings of famous scenes from Greek history, beginning with the destruction of Troy and including other legendary events such as the battle with the Amazons. Over 20 years after the Battle of Marathon, scenes from that conflict were added to the Stoa. The paintings were executed on large wooden panels by some of the leading artists of the day, including Polygnotus, Micon, and Panaenus.

Unfortunately, the paintings do not survive, and the structure is still in the process of archaeological excavation, but the ancient writer Pausanius did record the subjects he saw depicted there. The Marathon panels, probably painted by Micon, received the following description:

> The Boeotians of Plataea and the Attic contingent are coming to grips with the barbarians; at this point the action is evenly balanced between both sides. In the inner part of the fight the barbarians are fleeing and pushing one another into the marsh; at the extreme end of the painting are the Phoenician ships and the Greeks killing the barbarians who are tumbling into them. In this picture are also shown Marathon, the hero after whom the plain is named, Theseus, represented as coming up from the earth, Athena and Herakles—the Marathonians, according to their own account, were the first to recognize Herakles as a god. Of the combatants, the most conspicuous in the picture is Callimachus, who was chosen by the Athenians to be polemarch, and of the generals, Miltiades.

It is also known that Datis and Artaphernes appeared in the paintings as did Cynegirus, the man (perhaps the brother of Aeschylus) who lost his hand while grabbing the stern of a ship. Above the battle scenes, the gods and goddesses appeared and looked down upon the mortals' strife. Pausanius even reports that one of the unnamed men in the painting was the poet Aeschylus himself.

The Stoa was a favorite meeting place in Athens where one could see street performers, such as jugglers and sword-swallowers, or encounter merchants and beggars. It was also known to be a site where philosophers and other teachers would give lectures. Among the most famous of them was Zeno of Citium, whose followers were called "Stoics" because they met at the Stoa. Accordingly, generations of Athenians saw the images of Marathon as a regular part of their daily lives.

The Parthenon, the famous temple of Athena on the Acropolis, stands as one of the greatest works of architecture in human history. After taking a leading role in the repulsion of the Persian invaders from Greece and asserting dominance over their allies, the Athenians achieved a level of wealth unprecedented in the Greek world. Such power, prestige, wealth, and pride all came together during the age of Pericles, who channeled it into art—and an art that not only proclaimed the glory of Athens but also expressed the noblest possibilities of human achievement.

Designed by architects Iktinos and Kallikrates, the Parthenon was built from marble specially quarried from Mount Pentelikon and carried to the site on roads built exclusively for that purpose. Its dimensions are vast: its columns alone stand 34 feet high. Designed to impress with its imposing size, the Parthenon was also meant to convey a sense of order and stability, qualities much admired in Athens after decades of war. The dimensions of the Parthenon are related by a mathematical formula known as the "golden section," in which the width of the structure is 1.618 times the height, or approximately 8:5, a ratio that Plato associated with the harmony of the cosmos.

Once the temple itself was erected, work began on a series of ornamental sculptures that adorned the pediments beneath the gable ends of the roof and the decorative bands of relief sculptures, called friezes, that were placed around the top of the walls. Designed and supervised by the sculptor Phidias, the Parthenon frieze depicts a series of battles between the noble, civilized Greeks and their barbarian enemies. In all there are exactly 192 figures on

Pericles is shown presiding over the building of temples in the Acropolis.

the frieze—exactly the same number as the men who perished at Marathon. Since the battle itself is not represented on the frieze, some modern scholars believe that the numerical correspondence is a mere coincidence. On the other hand, Marathon had already attained great symbolic significance as the battle that made possible the glorious present under which the citizens of Periclean Athens were currently living. It is therefore not unreasonable to suppose that this pivotal battle should be commemorated on the city's greatest temple.

These fifth century masterworks would all command attention solely on the basis of their artistic merit even if they had nothing to do with the Battle of Marathon. Yet it is appropriate that they should be linked to this "battle that changed the world." The legacy of Marathon is, in many ways, the legacy of Greece itself: a stunning synthesis of humanism and idealism—the belief in the worth and dignity of human beings and in man's ability to shape his destiny and attain the most noble of aspirations. At the same time, there is the recognition of humankind's limitations and the tragic consequences that can result if people go astray. The valor of a soldier fighting for both freedom and honor and the arrogance of a person who fights for his or her own aggrandizement, a politician working toward the common good through democratic means and a despot whose ambition has little regard for anyone but himself—these are the opposing forces that the Greeks saw in the conflict at Marathon and that they universalized through their art. Through both words and stone, they speak to us across the millennia: The experience at Marathon helped make Greece believe that all things were possible if opportunities were used wisely. Its enduring legacy is the knowledge that they are still possible today.

All dates are Before the Common Era

c. 1200	Trojan War
c. 750–700	Homer's *Iliad* and *Odyssey*
683/2	Athens establishes annual elections for archon
594/3	Archonship of Solon of Athens
560–546	Croesus rules in Lydia
546	Cyrus conquers Croesus
557–530	Cyrus the Great is king of Persia
555	The elder Miltiades is sent to the Chersonesus
546–527	Pisistratus is tyrant of Athens
530	Reign of Cambyses

c.750–700
Homer's *Iliad*
and *Odyssey*

c.800

650

Timeline

527–510	Hippias is tyrant of Athens
521–486	Darius is king of Persia
520–490	Cleomenes is king of Sparta
513	Darius mounts his Scythian campaign
510	Expulsion of Hippias from Athens
508/7	Archonship of Cleisthenes in Athens
499–494	Ionian Revolt
490	Persian campaign against Athens and Eretria, Battle of Marathon
489	Miltiades fails to capture Paros, dies in prison
485	Birth of Herodotus
493/2	Archonship of Themistocles, who built the Athenian navy

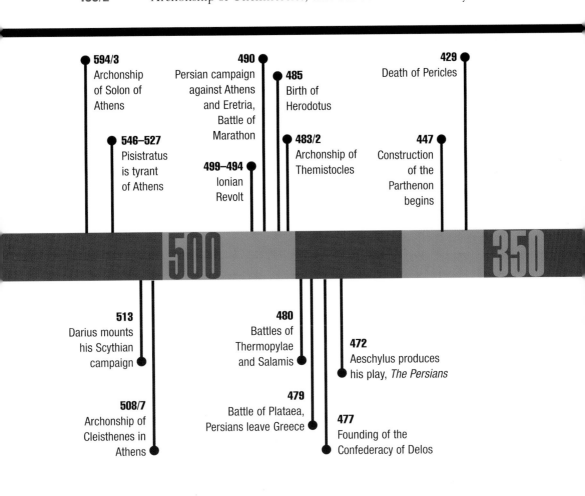

594/3
Archonship of Solon of Athens

546–527
Pisistratus is tyrant of Athens

490
Persian campaign against Athens and Eretria, Battle of Marathon

499–494
Ionian Revolt

485
Birth of Herodotus

483/2
Archonship of Themistocles

429
Death of Pericles

447
Construction of the Parthenon begins

500

350

513
Darius mounts his Scythian campaign

508/7
Archonship of Cleisthenes in Athens

480
Battles of Thermopylae and Salamis

479
Battle of Plataea, Persians leave Greece

472
Aeschylus produces his play, *The Persians*

477
Founding of the Confederacy of Delos

480–479	Xerxes attacks Greece
480	Battles of Thermopylae and Salamis
479	Battle of Plataea, Persians leave Greece
477	Founding of the Confederacy of Delos
472	Aeschylus produces his play, *The Persians*
465	Death of Xerxes
463	Political career of Pericles begins with prosecution of Cimon
459–446	First Peloponesian War
447	Construction of the Parthenon begins
431–404	Second Peloponesian War
429	Death of Pericles

Aeschylus. *The Persians*, tr. Lembke and Herington. Oxford: Oxford University Press, 1981.

Bowder, Diana. *Who Was Who in the Greek World.* New York: Washington Square Press, 1982.

Bury, J.B. *A History of Greece.* New York: St. Martin's Press, 1985.

Crawford, Michael and David Whitehead. *Archaic and Classical Greece.* Cambridge: Cambridge University Press, 1983.

Fowler, Barbara Hughes, ed. and trans. *Archaic Greek Poetry.* Madison: University of Wisconsin Press, 1992.

Green, Peter. *The Greco-Persian Wars.* Berkeley: University of California Press, 1996.

Hanson, Victor Davis. *The Wars of the Ancient Greeks.* London: Cassell, 1999.

Herodotus. *The Histories*, tr. Robin Waterfield. Oxford: Oxford University Press, 1998.

Lefkowitz, Mary R. *The Lives of the Greek Poets.* Baltimore: Johns Hopkins University Press, 1981.

Nepos, Cornelius. *Great Generals of Foreign Nations*, tr. J.C. Rolfe. Cambridge: Harvard University Press, 1999.

Osborne, Robin. *Archaic and Classical Greek Art.* Oxford: Oxford University Press, 1998

Oxford History of the Classical World, eds. Boardman, Griffin, and Murray. Oxford: Oxford University Press, 1986.

Simonides. *Greek Lyric*, tr. David Campbell. Cambridge: Harvard University Press, 1991.

page:

2: Reprint from "Encyclopedia of the Ancient Greek World," map by Margaret Brenson
6: Wolfgang Kaehler/Corbis
9: Scala/Art Resource
17: Reunion des Musees Nationaux/ Art Resource, NY
13: Erich Lessing/Art Resource, NY
39: SEF/Art Resource, NY
20: Giraudon/Art Resource, NY
24: Reprint from "Who Was Who in the Greek World," Diana Bowder, Ed.
58: Bettmann/Corbis
62: Bettmann/Corbis
64: Bettmann/Corbis
75: Bettmann/Corbis
68: Vanni Archive/Corbis
67: Reprint from "Wars of the Ancient Greeks," map by Arcadia Editions Ltd.

79: Bettmann/Corbis
36: Hulton/Archive
29: Gianni Dagli Orti/Corbis
34: Bettmann/Corbis
46: Reunion des Musees Nationaux, Art Resource, NY
51: Hulton Archive by Getty Images
40: Erich Lessing/Art Resource, NY
41: Erich Lessing/Art Resource, NY
44: Gianni Dagli Orti/Corbis
53: Reprinted from "Cambridge Illustrated History of Ancient Greece," map by European Map Graphics Ltd.
82: SEF/Art Resource, NY
76: Eric and David Hosking/Corbis
84: Bettmann/Corbis

Cover: Bettmann/Corbis

Frontis: Reprinted from *Encyclopedia of the Ancient Greek World*, David Sachs, map by Margaret Brenson, Facts on File, 1995.

DAVID J. CALIFF received his Ph.D. from the University of Wisconsin–Madison and currently teaches Latin and English literature at the Academy of Notre Dame in Villanova, Pennsylvania. A published Latin poet, he is the author of *A Guide to Latin Meter and Verse Composition* and articles on classical poetry and ancient Greek literary criticism. As a hobby, he gives college tours at New York's Metropolitan Museum of Art in conjunction with Kean University.